Land, W

by Le

PEARSON
Scott
Foresman

DK

What makes up Earth?

Land and water cover the Earth.

There is more water than land.

Earth has different kinds of land.

Earth has different kinds of water.

Kinds of Land and Water

A plain is flat land.

A hill is land that gets higher.

A lake is water with land all around it.

A river is water that flows through land.

River

Hill

Plain

Lake

What are rocks and soil?

Rocks are nonliving things.

Rocks can be many colors, sizes, and shapes.

Big rocks are called boulders.

Sand is tiny pieces of broken rock.

Rocks are a natural resource.

They come from Earth.

A **natural resource** is a part
of Earth.

A natural resource is a useful thing.

Soil

Soil is a natural resource.

Soil can be made of sand, clay, and humus.

Sand is rough and loose.

Clay is sticky and soft.

Humus is made of parts of living things that died.

Sand

Clay

Humus

Worms help make soil loose.

Loose soil helps plants grow.

Humus in soil helps plants grow.

What changes land?

Weathering is when rocks break and change.

Wind, water, and ice cause weathering.

It can change the size, shape, and color of rocks.

Erosion can change land too.

Erosion is when rocks and soil move.

Wind or water causes erosion.

Plant roots hold soil in place.

This can slow down erosion.

How do living things use natural resources?

Air is a natural resource.

Plants and trees need air.

Some animals fly in the air.

People and animals breathe air.

Using Water

Living things use water.

Water is a natural resource.

Using Land

Land is a natural resource.

People grow food on land.

Trees grow on land.

People use wood to build things.

Minerals come from the land.

Minerals are in rocks and soil.

Copper is a mineral.

People use copper to make pennies.

How can you reduce, reuse, and recycle?

Help save land, water, and air.

Reduce how much you use.

Reuse things again and again.

Recycle old things into new things.

Living things use natural resources.
Natural resources come from Earth.
We need the land, air, and water
of Earth.

Glossary

clay   a sticky, soft part of soil

erosion   when wind or water moves
                                  rocks and soil

humus   a part of soil made of parts
                                  of living things that died

minerals   nonliving things found in
                                  rocks and soil

natural resource   a useful thing that comes
                                  from nature

rocks   nonliving things that come
                                  from Earth

sand   tiny pieces of broken rock

weathering   when rocks break apart
                                  and change